JONES & BARTLETT LEARNING INFORMATION SYSTEMS SECURITY & ASSURANCE SERIES

LABORATORY MANUAL TO ACCOMPANY

Managing Risk in Information Systems

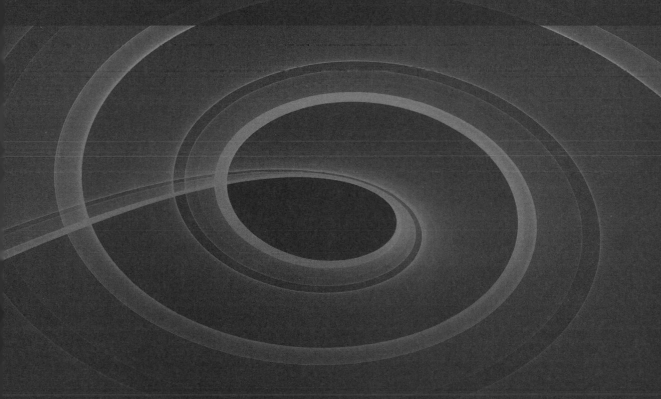

vLAB
SOLUTIONS

JONES & BARTLETT
LEARNING

World Headquarters
Jones & Bartlett Learning
5 Wall Street
Burlington, MA 01803
978-443-5000
info@jblearning.com
www.jblearning.com

Jones & Bartlett Learning books and products are available through most bookstores and online booksellers. To contact Jones & Bartlett Learning directly, call 800-832-0034, fax 978-443-8000, or visit our website, www.jblearning.com.

This publication is designed to provide accurate and authoritative information in regard to the subject matter covered. It is sold with the understanding that the publisher is not engaged in rendering legal, accounting, or other professional service. If legal advice or other expert assistance is required, the service of a competent professional person should be sought.

Production Credits
Chief Executive Officer: Ty Field
President: James Homer
SVP, Chief Operating Officer: Don Jones, Jr.
SVP, Chief Technology Officer: Dean Fossella
SVP, Chief Marketing Officer: Alison M. Pendergast
SVP, Curriculum Solutions: Christopher Will
VP, Design and Production: Anne Spencer
VP, Manufacturing and Inventory Control: Therese Connell
Author: vLab Solutions, LLC, David Kim, President
Editorial Management: Perspectives, Inc., Phil Graham, President
Reprints and Special Projects Manager: Susan Schultz
Associate Production Editor: Tina Chen
Director of Marketing: Alisha Weisman
Senior Marketing Manager: Andrea DeFronzo
Cover Design: Anne Spencer
Composition: vLab Solutions, LLC
Cover Image: © ErickN/ShutterStock, Inc.
Printing and Binding: Malloy, Inc.
Cover Printing: Malloy, Inc.

ISBN: 978-1-4496-4396-6

6048
Printed in the United States of America
15 14 13   10 9 8 7 6 5 4 3

Table of Contents

Current Version Date: 05/30/2011

Laboratory #1

Lab 1: How to Identify Threats & Vulnerabilities in an IT Infrastructure

Learning Objectives and Outcomes

Upon completing this lab, students will be able to:

- Identify common risks, threats, and vulnerabilities found throughout the seven domains of a typical IT infrastructure

- Align risks, threats, and vulnerabilities to one of the seven domains of a typical IT infrastructure

- Given a scenario, prioritize risks, threats, and vulnerabilities based on their risk impact to the organization from a risk assessment perspective

- Prioritize the identified critical, major, and minor risks, threats, and software vulnerabilities found throughout the seven domains of a typical IT infrastructure

Required Setup and Tools

This is a paper-based lab and does not require the use of the ISS "mock" IT infrastructure or virtualized server farm.

The standard Instructor and Student VM workstation with Microsoft Office 2007 or higher is required for this lab. Students will need access to Lab #1 – Assessment Worksheet Part A (a list of 21 risks, threats, and vulnerabilities commonly found in an IT infrastructure) and must identify which of the seven domains of a typical IT infrastructure the risk, threat, or vulnerability impacts.

In addition, Microsoft Word is a required tool for the student to craft an executive summary for management summarizing the findings and alignment of the identified risks, threats, and vulnerabilities that were found.

Recommended Procedures

Lab #1 – Student Steps:

Student steps needed to perform Lab #1 – Identify Threats and Vulnerabilities in an IT Infrastructure:

1. Connect your removable hard drive or USB hard drive to a classroom workstation.
2. Boot up your classroom workstation and DHCP for an IP host address.
3. Login to your classroom workstation and enable Microsoft Word.
4. Review Figure 1 – Seven Domains of a Typical IT Infrastructure.

Current Version Date: 05/30/2011

5. Discuss how risk can impact each of the seven domains of a typical IT infrastructure: User, Workstation, LAN, LAN-to-WAN, WAN, Remote Access, Systems/Applications Domains.

6. Work on Lab #1 – Assessment Worksheet Part A. Part A is a matching exercise that requires the students to align the risk, threat, or vulnerability with one of the seven domains of a typical IT infrastructure where there is a risk impact or risk factor to consider. Students may work in small groups of two or three.

7. Have the students perform Lab #1 – Assessment Worksheet

8. Answer Lab #1 – Assessment Questions and submit.

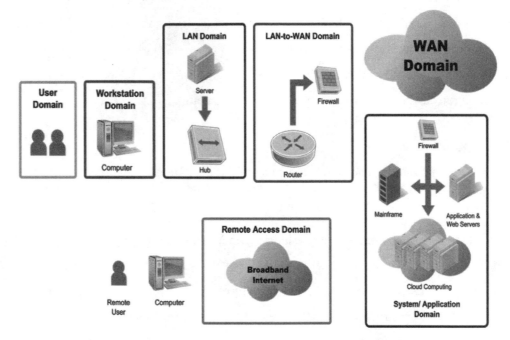

Figure 1 – Seven Domains of a Typical IT Infrastructure

Deliverables

Upon completion of Lab #1 – Identify Threats and Vulnerabilities in an IT Infrastructure, students are required to provide the following deliverables as part of this lab:

1. Lab #1 – Assessment Worksheet Part A. Identification and mapping of 21 risks, threats, and vulnerabilities to the seven domains of a typical IT infrastructure

2. Lab #1 - Assessment Questions and Answers

Current Version Date: 05/30/2011

Evaluation Criteria and Rubrics

The following are the evaluation criteria and rubrics for Lab #1 that the students must perform:

1. Was the student able to identify common risks, threats, and vulnerabilities found throughout the seven domains of a typical IT infrastructure? – **[25%]**

2. Was the student able to align risks, threats, and vulnerabilities to one of the seven domains of a typical IT infrastructure accurately? – **[25%]**

3. Given a scenario in Part A, was the student able to prioritize risks, threats, and vulnerabilities based on their risk impact to the organization? – **[25%]**

4. Was the student able to prioritize the identified critical, major, and minor risks, threats, and software vulnerabilities? – **[25%]**

Current Version Date: 05/30/2011

Lab #1: Assessment Worksheet

Part A – List of Risks, Threats, and Vulnerabilities

Commonly Found in an IT Infrastructure

Course Name: _____

Student Name: _____

Instructor Name: _____

Lab Due Date: _____

Overview

The following risks, threats, and vulnerabilities were found in a healthcare IT infrastructure servicing patients with life-threatening situations. Given the list, select which of the seven domains of a typical IT infrastructure is primarily impacted by the risk, threat, or vulnerability.

Risk – Threat – Vulnerability	Primary Domain Impacted
Unauthorized access from public Internet	
User destroys data in application and deletes all files	
Hacker penetrates your IT infrastructure and gains access to your internal network	
Intra-office employee romance gone bad	
Fire destroys primary data center	
Communication circuit outages	
Workstation OS has a known software vulnerability	
Unauthorized access to organization owned	
Workstations	
Loss of production data	
Denial of service attack on organization e-mail Server	

Current Version Date: 05/30/2011

Risk – Threat – Vulnerability	Primary Domain Impacted
Remote communications from home office	
LAN server OS has a known software vulnerability	
User downloads an unknown e –mail attachment	
Workstation browser has software vulnerability	
Service provider has a major network outage	
Weak ingress/egress traffic filtering degrades Performance	
User inserts CDs and USB hard drives with personal photos, music, and videos on organization owned computers	
VPN tunneling between remote computer and ingress/egress router	
WLAN access points are needed for LAN connectivity within a warehouse	
Need to prevent rogue users from unauthorized WLAN access	

Current Version Date: 05/30/2011

Lab #1: Assessment Worksheet

Identify Threats and Vulnerabilities in an IT Infrastructure

Course Name: _____

Student Name: _____

Instructor Name: _____

Lab Due Date: _____

Overview

One of the most important first steps to risk management and implementing a risk mitigation strategy is to identify known risks, threats, and vulnerabilities and organize them. The purpose of the seven domains of a typical IT infrastructure is to help organize the roles, responsibilities, and accountabilities for risk management and risk mitigation. This lab requires students to identify risks, threats, and vulnerabilities and map them to the domain that these impact from a risk management perspective.

Lab Assessment Questions

Given the scenario of a healthcare organization, answer the following Lab #1 assessment questions from a risk management perspective:

1. Healthcare organizations are under strict compliance to HIPPA privacy requirements which require that an organization have proper security controls for handling personal healthcare information (PHI) privacy data. This includes security controls for the IT infrastructure handling PHI privacy data. Which one of the listed risks, threats, or vulnerabilities can violate HIPPA privacy requirements? List one and justify your answer in one or two sentences.

2. How many threats and vulnerabilities did you find that impacted risk within each of the seven domains of a typical IT infrastructure?

   User Domain:

   Workstation Domain:

   LAN Domain:

   LAN-to-WAN Domain:

   WAN Domain:

Current Version Date: 05/30/2011

Remote Access Domain:

Systems/Application Domain:

3. Which domain(s) had the greatest number of risks, threats, and vulnerabilities?

4. What is the risk impact or risk factor (critical, major, minor) that you would qualitatively assign to the risks, threats, and vulnerabilities you identified for the LAN-to-WAN Domain for the healthcare and HIPPA compliance scenario?

5. Of the three Systems/Application Domain risks, threats, and vulnerabilities identified, which one requires a disaster recovery plan and business continuity plan to maintain continued operations during a catastrophic outage?

6. Which domain represents the greatest risk and uncertainty to an organization?

7. Which domain requires stringent access controls and encryption for connectivity to corporate resources from home?

8. Which domain requires annual security awareness training and employee background checks for sensitive positions to help mitigate risk from employee sabotage?

9. Which domains need software vulnerability assessments to mitigate risk from software vulnerabilities?

10. Which domain requires AUPs to minimize unnecessary User initiated Internet traffic and can be monitored and controlled by web content filters?

Current Version Date: 05/30/2011

11. In which domain do you implement web content filters?

12. If you implement a wireless LAN (WLAN) to support connectivity for laptops in the Workstation Domain, which domain does WLAN fall within?

13. A bank under Gramm-Leach-Bliley-Act (GLBA) for protecting customer privacy has just implemented their online banking solution allowing customers to access their accounts and perform transactions via their computer or PDA device. Online banking servers and their public Internet hosting would fall within which domains of security responsibility?

14. Customers that conduct online banking using their laptop or personal computer must use HTTPS:, the secure and encrypted version of HTTP: browser communications. HTTPS:// encrypts webpage data inputs and data through the public Internet and decrypts that webpage and data once displayed on your browser. True or False.

15. Explain how a layered security strategy throughout the 7-domains of a typical IT infrastructure can help mitigate risk exposure for loss of privacy data or confidential data from the Systems/Application Domain.

Current Version Date: 05/30/2011

Laboratory #2

Lab 2: Align Risk, Threats, & Vulnerabilities to COBIT P09 Risk Management Controls

Learning Objectives and Outcomes

Upon completing this lab, students will be able to:

- Define what COBIT (Control Objectives for Information and related Technology) P09 Risk Management is for an IT infrastructure

- Describe the 6 control objectives of COBIT P09 which are used as benchmarks for IT risk assessment and risk management

- Relate how threats and vulnerabilities align to the COBIT PO9 Risk Management definition for the assessment and management of IT risk

- Use the COBIT PO9 controls as a guide to define the scope of risk management for an IT infrastructure

- Apply the COBIT PO9 controls to help plan and organize the identified IT risks, threats, and vulnerabilities and the on-going management and remediation operation requirements

Required Setup and Tools

This is a paper-based lab. A PDF copy of the COBIT v4.1 Framework from ISACA is needed for this paper-based lab. ISACA is the global organization that defines the roles of information systems governance, security, audit and assurance professionals worldwide through its Certified Information Systems Auditor (CISA) and Certified Information Security Manager (CISM) professional certifications. ISACA's website is: www.isaca.org.

The standard Instructor and Student VM workstation with Microsoft Office 2007 or higher is required for this lab. Students will be required to answer the Lab #2 – Assessment Worksheet questions as part of this lab.

Recommended Procedures

Lab #2 – Student Steps:

Student steps needed to perform Lab #2 – Align Risk, Threats, & Vulnerabilities to the COBIT Risk Management Controls:

1. Connect your removable hard drive or USB hard drive to a classroom workstation.

2. Boot up your classroom workstation and DHCP for an IP host address.

Current Version Date: 05/30/2011

3. Login to your classroom workstation and enable Microsoft Word.

4. Conduct a high-level narrative discussion and review of the COBIT v4.1 Framework.

5. Review the COBIT P09 Control Objective definition, scope, and focus areas for assessing and managing IT risk.

6. Relate how the COBIT (P09) Control Objective definition relates to assessing and managing IT risk within each of the seven domains of a typical IT infrastructure: User, Workstation, LAN, LAN-to-WAN, WAN, Remote Access, Systems/Applications Domains

7. Explore the structure and format of how to align risks, threats, and vulnerabilities identified from your IT infrastructure to the COBIT P09 Control Objective definition, scope, and focus areas Information, Applications, Infrastructure, and People.

8. Explore the hierarchy for assessing and managing IT risks:

   - Step #1: Align the risk, threat or vulnerability assessment to **C-I-A primary first and assess**

   - Step #2: Align the risk, threat, or vulnerability remediation to **Effectiveness, Efficiency, Compliance, and Reliability secondary**

   - Step #3: Assess the risk impact for each threat or vulnerability in the following focus areas:

     o **Information** – What is the risk impact? How can this be mitigated? How can this be managed?

     o **Applications** – What is the risk impact? How can this be mitigated? How can this be managed?

     o **Infrastructure** – What is the risk impact? How can this be mitigated? How can this be managed?

     o **People** – What is the risk impact? How can this be mitigated? How can this be managed?

9. Using the list of identified threats and vulnerabilities that were identified from the Lab #1 – How to Identify Threats and Vulnerabilities in Your IT Infrastructure, align the high, medium, and low vulnerabilities to the COBIT (P09) Risk Management control objectives for assessing and managing risk. See Lab #2 – Assessment Worksheet - Part A - COBIT (P09) Alignment.

10. Answer Lab #2 – Assessment Questions.

Deliverables

Upon completion of the Lab #2 – Align Risk, Threats, & Vulnerabilities to the COBIT Risk Management Controls, students are required to provide the following deliverables as part of this lab:

1. Lab #2 – Assessment Questions and Answers. This will include details about using the COBIT (P09) assessment and risk management approach for the identified vulnerabilities from Lab #1

Evaluation Criteria and Rubrics

The following are the evaluation criteria and rubrics for Lab #2 that the students must perform:

1. Was the student able to define what COBIT (Control Objectives for Information and related Technology) P09 Risk Management is for an IT infrastructure? – [**20%**]

2. Was the student able to describe the 6 control objectives of COBIT P09 which are used as benchmarks for IT risk assessment and risk management? – [**20%**]

3. Was the student able to relate how threats and vulnerabilities align to the COBIT PO9 Risk Management definition for the assessment and management of IT risk? – [**20%**]

4. Was the student able to use the COBIT PO9 controls as a guide to define the scope of risk management for an IT infrastructure? – [**20%**]

5. Was the student able to apply the COBIT PO9 controls to help plan and organize the identified IT risks, threats, and vulnerabilities and the on-going management and remediation operation requirements? – [**20%**]

Current Version Date: 05/30/2011

Lab #2: Assessment Worksheet

Align Risk, Threats, & Vulnerabilities to COBIT P09 Risk Management Controls

Course Name: _____

Student Name: _____

Instructor Name: _____

Lab Due Date: _____

Overview

Think of the COBIT framework as a giant checklist for what an IT or Risk Management auditors would do if they were going to audit how your organization approaches risk management for your IT infrastructure. COBIT P09 defines 6 control objectives for assessing and managing IT risk within four different focus areas.

The first lab task is to align your identified threats and vulnerabilities from Lab #1 – How to Identify Threats and Vulnerabilities in Your IT Infrastructure.

Lab Assessment Questions

1. From the identified threats & vulnerabilities from Lab #1 – (List At Least 3 and No More than 5, High/Medium/Low Nessus Risk Factor Definitions for Vulnerabilities)

   a.

   b.

   c.

   d.

   e.

2. For the above identified threats and vulnerabilities, which of the following COBIT P09 Risk Management control objectives are affected?

   • PO9.1 IT Risk Management Framework –

   • PO9.2 Establishment of Risk Context –

Current Version Date: 05/30/2011

- PO9.3 Event Identification –

- PO9.4 Risk Assessment –

- PO9.5 Risk Response –

- PO9.6 Maintenance and Monitoring of a Risk Action Plan –

3. From the identified threats & vulnerabilities from Lab #1 – (List At Least 3 and No More than 5), specify whether the threat or vulnerability impacts confidentiality – integrity – availability:

	Confidentiality	Integrity	Availability
a.			
b.			
c.			
d.			
e.			

4. For each of the threats and vulnerabilities from Lab #1 (List at Least 3 and No More than 5) that you have remediated, what must you assess as part of your overall COBIT P09 risk management approach for your IT infrastructure?

5. For each of the threats and vulnerabilities from Lab #1 – (List at Least 3 and No More than 5) assess the risk impact or risk factor that it has on your organization in the following areas and explain how this risk can be mitigated and managed:

a. Threat or Vulnerability #1:
   o **Information** –
   o **Applications** –
   o **Infrastructure** –
   o **People** –
b. Threat or Vulnerability #2:
   o **Information** –
   o **Applications** –
   o **Infrastructure** –

Current Version Date: 05/30/2011

      o **People** –

  c. Threat or Vulnerability #3:

      o **Information** –

      o **Applications** –

      o **Infrastructure** –

      o **People** –

  d. Threat or Vulnerability #4:

      o **Information** –

      o **Applications** –

      o **Infrastructure** –

      o **People** –

  e. Threat or Vulnerability #5:

      o **Information** –

      o **Applications** –

      o **Infrastructure** –

      o **People** –

6. True or False – COBIT P09 Risk Management controls objectives focus on assessment and management of IT risk.

7. Why is it important to address each identified threat or vulnerability from a C-I-A perspective?

8. When assessing the risk impact a threat or vulnerability has on your "information" assets, why must you align this assessment with your Data Classification Standard? How can a Data Classification Standard help you assess the risk impact on your "information" assets?

9. When assessing the risk impact a threat or vulnerability has on your "application" and "infrastructure", why must you align this assessment with both a server and application software vulnerability assessment and remediation plan?

Current Version Date: 05/30/2011

10. When assessing the risk impact a threat or vulnerability has on your "people", we are concerned with users and employees within the User Domain as well as the IT security practitioners who must implement the risk mitigation steps identified. How can you communicate to your end-user community that a security threat or vulnerability has been identified for a production system or application? How can you prioritize risk remediation tasks?

11. What is the purpose of using the COBIT risk management framework and approach?

12. What is the difference between effectiveness versus efficiency when assessing risk and risk management?

13. Which three of the seven focus areas pertaining to IT risk management are primary focus areas of risk assessment and risk management and directly relate to information systems security?

14. Why is it important to assess risk impact from four different perspectives as part of the COBIT P.09 Framework?

15. What is the name of the organization who defined the COBIT P.09 Risk Management Framework Definition?

Current Version Date: 05/30/2011

Laboratory #3

Lab 3: Define the Scope & Structure for an IT Risk Management Plan

Learning Objectives and Outcomes

Upon completing this lab, students will be able to:

- Define the purpose and objectives of an IT risk management plan

- Define the scope and boundary for an IT risk management plan to encompass the seven domains of a typical IT infrastructure

- Relate identified risks, threats, and vulnerabilities to an IT risk management plan and risk areas

- Incorporate the five major parts of an IT risk management process into the table of contents of the plan

- Craft an IT risk management plan table of contents that addresses the seven domains of a typical IT infrastructure and the five major parts of risk management and risk areas

Required Setup and Tools

This is a paper-based lab and does not require the use of a "mock" IT infrastructure or virtualized server farm.

The standard Instructor and Student VM workstation with Microsoft Office 2007 or higher is required for this lab for Internet access and Microsoft Word for answering and submitting the Lab #3 – Assessment Worksheet questions.

The risks, threats, and vulnerabilities identified in Lab #1 – Identify Threats & Vulnerabilities in an IT Infrastructure will be used as a basis for the scenario in Lab #3. Students are to focus their IT risk management plan table of contents using one of the scenarios and vertical industries assigned by the Instructor.

In addition, Microsoft Word is a required tool for the student to craft an IT risk management plan table of contents. The scope and structure of the table of contents will be presented by the Instructor in the demo overview lab.

Recommended Procedures

Lab #3 – Student Steps:

Student steps needed to perform Lab #3 – Define the Scope & Structure for an IT Risk Management Plan:

1. Connect your removable hard drive or USB hard drive to a classroom workstation.

2. Boot up your classroom workstation and DHCP for an IP host address.

3. Login to your classroom workstation and enable Microsoft Word.

4. Review the risks within each of the seven domains from a risk management perspective – classroom discussion and interaction.

5. Review the 21 identified risks, threats, and vulnerabilities categorized within one of the seven domains of a typical IT infrastructure. Refer to your Lab #1 – Assessment Worksheet, Part A – List of Identified Risks, Threats, and Vulnerabilities.

6. For each of the seven domains incorporate the following outline within the scope of your risk management plan table of contents:

   • Risk planning

   • Risk identification

   • Risk assessment

   • Risk mitigation

   • Risk monitoring

7. Obtain your scenario and vertical industry assignment from your Instructor.

8. Work with your group members to delegate various parts of your IT risk management plan.

9. Craft a comprehensive IT risk management plan table of contents using Microsoft Word. Be sure to encompass the four major risk areas identified in step #6 above.

10. Answer Lab #3 – Assessment Questions and ask your Instructor questions for guidance.

Deliverables

Upon completion of the Lab 3# - Define the Scope & Structure for an IT Risk Management Plan, students are required to provide the following deliverables as part of this lab:

1. Lab #3 – IT Risk Management Plan Table of Contents

2. Lab #3 - Assessment Worksheet Questions and Answers

Current Version Date: 05/30/2011

Evaluation Criteria and Rubrics

The following are the evaluation criteria and rubrics for Lab #3 that the students must perform:

1. Was the student able to define the purpose and objectives of an IT risk management plan? – **[20%]**

2. Was the student able to define the scope and boundary for an IT risk management plan to encompass the seven domains of a typical IT infrastructure? – **[20%]**

3. Was the student able to relate identified risks, threats, and vulnerabilities to an IT risk management plan and risk areas? – **[20%]**

4. Was the student able to incorporate the five major parts of an IT risk management process into the table of contents of the plan? – **[20%]**

5. Was the student able to craft an IT risk management plan table of contents that addresses the seven domains of a typical IT infrastructure and the five major parts of risk management and risk areas? – **[20%]**

Current Version Date: 05/30/2011

Lab #3: Assessment Worksheet

Define the Scope & Structure for an IT Risk Management Plan

Course Name: _____

Student Name: _____

Instructor Name: _____

Lab Due Date: _____

Overview

The Instructor will assign your group one of the following scenarios and industry verticals. You must align your IT risk management plan from this scenario and industry vertical perspective along with any compliance law requirements.

1. Circle the scenario and industry vertical your Instructor assigned to your group:
    a. Healthcare provider under HIPPA compliance law
    b. Regional bank under GLBA compliance law
    c. Nationwide retailer under PCI DSS standard requirements
    d. Higher-education institution under FERPA compliance law
2. Make sure your table of contents addresses your scenario and vertical industry.
3. Make sure your table of contents includes at a minimum, the five major parts of IT risk management:
    *   Risk planning
    *   Risk identification
    *   Risk assessment
    *   Risk mitigation
    *   Risk monitoring
4. Make sure your table of contents is executive management ready and addresses all the risk topics and issues needed for executive management awareness.
5. Answer Lab #3 – Assessment Worksheet questions and submit as part of your Lab #3 deliverables.

Current Version Date: 05/30/2011

Lab #3: Assessment Worksheet

Define the Scope & Structure for an IT Risk Management Plan

Course Name: _____

Student Name: _____

Instructor Name: _____

Lab Due Date: _____

Overview

Answer the following Lab #3 – Assessment Worksheet questions pertaining to your IT risk management plan design and table of contents.

Lab Assessment Questions

1. What is the goal or objective of an IT risk management plan?

2. What are the five fundamental components of an IT risk management plan?

3. Define what risk planning is.

4. What is the first step in performing risk management?

5. What is the exercise called when you are trying to identify an organization's risk health?

6. What practice helps reduce or eliminate risk?

7. What on-going practice helps track risk in real-time?

Current Version Date: 05/30/2011

8. Given that an IT risk management plan can be large in scope, why is it a good idea to development a risk management plan team?

9. Within the seven domains of a typical IT infrastructure, which domain is the most difficult to plan, identify, assess, remediate, and monitor?

10. From your scenario perspective, with which compliance law or standard does your organization have to comply? How did this impact the scope and boundary of your IT risk management plan?

11. How did the risk identification and risk assessment of the identified risks, threats, and vulnerabilities contribute to your IT risk management plan table of contents?

12. What risks, threats, and vulnerabilities did you identify and assess that require immediate risk mitigation given the criticality of the threat or vulnerability?

13. For risk monitoring, what techniques or tools can you implement within each of the seven domains of a typical IT infrastructure to help mitigate risk?

14. For risk mitigation, what processes and procedures are needed to help streamline and implement risk mitigation solutions to the production IT infrastructure?

15. How does risk mitigation impact change control management and vulnerability management?

Current Version Date: 05/30/2011

Laboratory #4

Lab 4: Perform a Qualitative Risk Assessment for an IT Infrastructure

Learning Objectives and Outcomes

Upon completing this lab, students will be able to:

- Define the purpose and objectives of an IT risk assessment

- Align identified risks, threats, and vulnerabilities to an IT risk assessment that encompasses the seven domains of a typical IT infrastructure

- Classify identified risks, threats, and vulnerabilities according to a qualitative risk assessment template

- Prioritize classified risks, threats, and vulnerabilities according to the defined qualitative risk assessment scale

- Craft an executive summary that addresses the risk assessment findings, risk assessment impact, and recommendations to remediate areas of non-compliance

Required Setup and Tools

This is a paper-based lab and does not require the use of a "mock" IT infrastructure or virtualized server farm.

The standard Instructor and Student VM workstation with Microsoft Office 2007 or higher is required for this lab for Internet access and Microsoft Word for answering and submitting the Lab #4 – Assessment Worksheet questions.

The risks, threats, and vulnerabilities identified in Lab #1 – Identify Threats & Vulnerabilities in an IT Infrastructure will be used as a basis for the scenario in Lab #4. Students are to focus their IT risk assessment using one of the scenarios and vertical industry examples assigned by the Instructor.

Students will use Microsoft Word to perform a qualitative risk assessment according to pre-defined, qualitative metrics and definitions. In addition, students will use Microsoft Word to document their performance of a qualitative risk assessment classifying the risk impact and prioritization for the identified risks, threats, and vulnerabilities.

Current Version Date: 05/30/2011

Recommended Procedures

Lab #4 – Student Steps:

Student steps needed to perform Lab #4 – Perform a Qualitative Risk Assessment for an IT Infrastructure:

1. Connect your removable hard drive or USB hard drive to a classroom workstation.

2. Boot up your classroom workstation and DHCP for an IP host address.

3. Login to your classroom workstation and enable Microsoft Word.

4. Review Figure 1 – Seven Domains of a Typical IT Infrastructure.

5. Identify the scenario/vertical industry assigned by your Instructor.

   a. Healthcare provider under HIPPA compliance law

   b. Regional bank under GLBA compliance law

   c. Nationwide retailer under PCI DSS standard requirements

   d. Higher-education institution under FERPA compliance law

6. Review the Lab #4 – Assessment Worksheet, Part A – Qualitative Assessment Risk Impact/ Risk Factor.

7. Perform a Qualitative Risk Assessment and assign a Risk Impact/Risk Factor for each of the identified risks, threats, and vulnerabilities using Lab #4 – Assessment Worksheet Part A.

8. Craft a four-paragraph executive summary according to the following outline:

   • Purpose of the risk assessment & summary of risks, threats, and vulnerabilities found throughout the IT infrastructure

   • Prioritization of critical, major, minor risk assessment elements

   • Risk assessment and risk impact summary

   • Recommendations and next steps

9. Work on Lab #4 – Assessment Questions and submit.

Deliverables

Upon completion of Lab #4 – Perform a Qualitative Risk Assessment for an IT Infrastructure, students are required to provide the following deliverables as part of this lab:

1. Lab #4 – Qualitative Risk Assessment Worksheet with assigned risk impact/risk factors for the identified domains of a typical IT infrastructure ("1" – Critical, "2" – Major, "3" – Minor)

2. Lab #4 – Qualitative Risk Assessment executive summary

3. Lab #4 - Assessment Questions and Answers

Current Version Date: 05/30/2011

Evaluation Criteria and Rubrics

The following are the evaluation criteria and rubrics for Lab #4 that the students must perform:

1. Was the student able to define the purpose and objectives of an IT risk assessment? – [**20%**]

2. Was the student able to align identified risks, threats, and vulnerabilities to an IT risk assessment that encompasses the seven domains of a typical IT infrastructure? – [**20%**]

3. Was the student able to classify identified risks, threats, and vulnerabilities according to a qualitative risk assessment template? – [**20%**]

4. Was the student able to prioritize classified risks, threats, and vulnerabilities according to the defined qualitative risk assessment scale? – [**20%**]

5. Was the student able to craft an executive summary that addresses the risk assessment findings, risk assessment impact, and recommendations to remediate areas of non-compliance? – [**20%**]

Current Version Date: 05/30/2011

Lab #4: Assessment Worksheet

Part A – Perform a Qualitative Risk Assessment for an IT Infrastructure

Course Name: _____

Student Name: _____

Instructor Name: _____

Lab Due Date: _____

Overview

The following risks, threats, and vulnerabilities were found in an IT infrastructure. Your Instructor will assign you one of four different scenarios and vertical industries each of which is under a unique compliance law.

1. Scenario/Vertical Industry:

   a. Healthcare provider under HIPPA compliance law

   b. Regional bank under GLBA compliance law

   c. Nationwide retailer under PCI DSS standard requirements

   d. Higher-education institution under FERPA compliance law

2. Given the list, perform a qualitative risk assessment by assigning a risk impact/risk factor to each of identified risks, threats, and vulnerabilities throughout the seven domains of a typical IT infrastructure that the risk, threat, or vulnerability resides.

Risk – Threat – Vulnerability	Primary Domain Impacted	Risk Impact/Factor
Unauthorized access from public Internet		
User destroys data in application and deletes all files		
Hacker penetrates your IT infrastructure and gains access to your internal network		
Intra-office employee romance gone bad		
Fire destroys primary data center		

Current Version Date: 05/30/2011

Risk – Threat – Vulnerability	Primary Domain Impacted	Risk Impact/Factor
Service provider SLA is not achieved		
Workstation OS has a known software vulnerability		
Unauthorized access to organization owned workstations		
Loss of production data		
Denial of service attack on organization DMZ and e-mail server		
Remote communications from home office		
LAN server OS has a known software vulnerability		
User downloads and clicks on an unknown		
Workstation browser has software vulnerability		
Mobile employee needs secure browser access to sales order entry system		
Service provider has a major network outage		
Weak ingress/egress traffic filtering degrades performance		
User inserts CDs and USB hard drives with personal photos, music, and videos on organization owned computers		
VPN tunneling between remote computer and ingress/egress router is needed		
WLAN access points are needed for LAN connectivity within a warehouse		
Need to prevent eavesdropping on WLAN due to customer privacy data access		
DoS/DDoS attack from the WAN/Internet		

Current Version Date: 05/30/2011

3. For each of the identified risks, threats, and vulnerabilities, prioritize them by listing a "1", "2", and "3" next to each risk, threat, vulnerability found within each of the seven domains of a typical IT infrastructure. "1" = Critical, "2" = Major, "3" = Minor. Define the following qualitative risk impact/risk factor metrics:

"1" Critical – a risk, threat, or vulnerability that impacts compliance (i.e., privacy law requirement for securing privacy data and implementing proper security controls, etc.) and places the organization in a position of increased liability.

"2" Major – a risk, threat, or vulnerability that impacts the C-I-A of an organization's intellectual property assets and IT infrastructure.

"3" Minor – a risk, threat, or vulnerability that can impact user or employee productivity or availability of the IT infrastructure.

User Domain Risk Impacts:

Workstation Domain Risk Impacts:

LAN Domain Risk Impacts:

LAN-to-WAN Domain Risk Impacts:

WAN Domain Risk Impacts:

Remote Access Domain Risk Impacts:

Systems/Applications Domain Risk Impacts:

Current Version Date: 05/30/2011

4. Craft an executive summary for management using the following 4-paragraph format. The executive summary must address the following topics:

- Paragraph #1: Summary of findings: risks, threats, and vulnerabilities found throughout the seven domains of a typical IT infrastructure

- Paragraph #2: Approach and prioritization of critical, major, minor risk assessment elements

- Paragraph #3: Risk assessment and risk impact summary to the seven domains of a typical IT infrastructure

- Paragraph #4: Recommendations and next steps for executive management

Current Version Date: 05/30/2011

Lab #4: Assessment Worksheet

Perform a Qualitative Risk Assessment for an IT Infrastructure

Course Name: _____

Student Name: _____

Instructor Name: _____

Lab Due Date: _____

Overview

Answer the following Lab #4 – Assessment Worksheet questions pertaining to your qualitative IT risk assessment you performed.

Lab Assessment Questions

1. What is the goal or objective of an IT risk assessment?

2. Why is it difficult to conduct a qualitative risk assessment for an IT infrastructure?

3. What was your rationale in assigning "1" risk impact/ risk factor value of "Critical" for an identified risk, threat, or vulnerability?

4. When you assembled all of the "1" and "2" and "3" risk impact/risk factor values to the identified risks, threats, and vulnerabilities, how did you prioritize the "1", "2", and "3" risk elements? What would you say to executive management in regards to your final recommended prioritization?

Current Version Date: 05/30/2011

5. Identify a risk mitigation solution for each of the following risk factors:

User downloads and clicks on an unknown e-mail attachment –

Workstation OS has a known software vulnerability –

Need to prevent eavesdropping on WLAN due to customer privacy data access –

Weak ingress/egress traffic filtering degrades performance –

DoS/DDoS attack from the WAN/Internet –

Remote access from home office –

Production server corrupts database –

Current Version Date: 05/30/2011

Laboratory #5

Lab 5: How to Identify Risks, Threats & Vulnerabilities in an IT Infrastructure Using ZeNmap GUI (Nmap) & Nessus® Reports

Learning Objectives and Outcomes

Upon completing this lab, students will be able to:

- Review a ZeNmap GUI (Nmap) network discovery and port scanning report and a Nessus® software vulnerability report from a risk management perspective

- Identify hosts, operating systems, services, applications, and open ports on devices from the ZeNmap GUI (Nmap) scan report from a risk management perspective

- Identify critical, major, and minor software vulnerabilities from the Nessus® vulnerability assessment scan report

- Assess the exploit potential of the identified software vulnerabilities by conducting a high-level risk impact by visiting the Common Vulnerabilities & Exposures (CVE) online listing of software vulnerabilities at http://cve.mitre.org/

- Craft an executive summary prioritizing the identified critical and major threats and vulnerabilities and their risk impact on the IT organization

Required Setup and Tools

This is a paper-based lab and does not require the use of a "mock" IT infrastructure or virtualized server farm.

The standard Instructor and Student VM workstation with Microsoft Office 2007 or higher is required for this lab. Students will need access to the Internet to correlate found software vulnerabilities on the IT infrastructure with the Common Vulnerabilities and Exposures (CVE) online listing located at: http://cve.mitre.org/.

In addition, Microsoft Word is a required tool for the student to craft an executive summary for management summarizing the findings from the ZeNmap GUI (Nmap) and Nessus® vulnerability assessment scan reports and for completing the lab assessment questions and answers.

Current Version Date: 05/30/2011

Recommended Procedures

Lab #5 – Student Steps:

Student steps needed to perform Lab #5 – Identify Threats & Vulnerabilities in an IT Infrastructure Using ZeNmap GUI (Nmap) & Nessus Reports:

1. Connect your removable hard drive or USB hard drive to a classroom workstation.

2. Boot up your classroom workstation and DHCP for an IP host address.

3. Login to your classroom workstation and enable Microsoft Word.

4. Review Figure 1 – Seven Domains of a Typical IT Infrastructure.

5. Load your workstation's browser and go to: http://cve.mitre.org/ .

6. Familiarize yourself with the CVE listing and search engine tool.

   - Load sample search criteria: "Microsoft XP 2003 Service Pack 1", "Cisco ASA 5505 Security +", etc.

7. Review the ZeNmap GUI (Nmap) network discovery and vulnerability assessment scan report and identify the following:

   - What was the date and time stamp of the Nmap host scan?

   - How many total tests or scripts ran during the scan?

   - A SYN stealth scan discovers all open ports on the targeted host. How many ports are open on the targeted host?

   - What ports are open on the targeted host?

   - What services/applications are on the targeted host?

   - What is the MAC layer address of the targeted host?

   - What OS is loaded on the targeted host?

   - How many router hops away is the targeted host?

   - Does the ZeNmap GUI (Nmap) scan report provide any information regarding to risk, threats, or vulnerabilities found?

   - What must you do to confirm or verify if the identified OS, software, application has the latest release and/or software updates and patches?

8. Review the Nessus vulnerability assessment scan report and identify the following:

   - What was the date and time stamp of the Nessus host scan?

   - How many total vulnerabilities were found per host?

   - Of these vulnerabilities, how many were open ports, high, medium, or low criticality vulnerabilities?

- What specific information was obtained regarding the targeted host:
  - Name:
  - Operating System:
- Does the Nessus vulnerability assessment scan report provide any information regarding to risk, threats, or vulnerabilities found?
- What must you do to confirm or verify if the identified OS, software, application has the latest release and/or software updates and patches?

9. Answer the Lab #5 – Assessment Questions and submit to the Instructor.

Deliverables

Upon completion of Lab #5 – Identify Risks, Threats & Vulnerabilities in an IT Infrastructure Using ZeNmap GUI (Nmap) & Nessus® Reports, students are required to provide the following deliverables as part of this lab:

1. Lab #5 – A four-paragraph executive summary written to executive management providing a summary of findings, risk impact to the IT asset and organization, and recommendations for next steps
2. Lab #5 - Assessment Questions and Answers

Evaluation Criteria and Rubrics

The following are the evaluation criteria and rubrics for Lab #5 that the students must perform:

1. Was the student able to review a ZeNmap GUI (Nmap) network discovery and port scanning report and a Nessus® software vulnerability report from a risk management perspective? – [20%]
2. Was the student able to identify hosts, operating systems, services, applications, and open ports on devices from the ZeNmap GUI (Nmap) scan report from a risk management perspective? – [20%]
3. Was the student able to identify critical, major, and minor software vulnerabilities from the Nessus® vulnerability assessment scan report? – [20%]
4. Was the student able to assess the exploit potential of the identified software vulnerabilities by conducting a high-level risk impact by visiting the Common Vulnerabilities & Exposures (CVE) online listing of software vulnerabilities at http://cve.mitre.org/ ? – [20%]
5. Was the student able to craft an executive summary prioritizing the identified critical and major threats and vulnerabilities and their risk impact on the IT organization? – [20%]

Current Version Date: 05/30/2011

Lab #5: Assessment Worksheet

Identify Threats and Vulnerabilities in an IT Infrastructure

Course Name: _____

Student Name: _____

Instructor Name: _____

Lab Due Date: _____

Overview

One of the most important first steps to risk management and implementing a security strategy is to identify all resources and hosts within the IT infrastructure. Once you identify the workstations and servers, you now must then find the threats and vulnerabilities found on these workstations and servers. Servers that support mission critical applications require security operations and management procedures to ensure C-I-A throughout. Servers that house customer privacy data or intellectual property require additional security controls to ensure the C-I-A of that data. This lab requires the students to identify threats and vulnerabilities found within the Workstation, LAN, and Systems/Applications Domains.

Lab Assessment Questions

1. What are the differences between ZeNmap GUI (Nmap) and Nessus?

2. Which scanning application is better for performing a network discovery reconnaissance probing of an IP network infrastructure?

3. Which scanning application is better for performing a software vulnerability assessment with suggested remediation steps?

4. How many total scripts (i.e., test scans) does the Intense Scan using ZenMap GUI perform?

Current Version Date: 05/30/2011

5. From the ZenMap GUI pdf report page 6, what ports and services are enabled on the Cisco Security Appliance device?

6. What is the source IP address of the Cisco Security Appliance device (refer to page 6 of the pdf report)?

7. How many IP hosts were identified in the Nessus® vulnerability scan? List them.

8. While Nessus provides suggestions for remediation steps, what else does Nessus provide that can help you assess the risk impact of the identified software vulnerability?

9. Are open ports necessarily a risk? Why or why not?

10. When you identify a known software vulnerability, where can you go to assess the risk impact of the software vulnerability?

11. If Nessus provides a pointer in the vulnerability assessment scan report to look up CVE-2009-3555 when using the CVE search listing, specify what this CVE is, what the potential exploits are, and assess the severity of the vulnerability.

12. Explain how the CVE search listing can be a tool for security practitioners and a tool for hackers.

13. What must an IT organization do to ensure that software updates and security patches are implemented timely?

Current Version Date: 05/30/2011

14. What would you define in a vulnerability management policy for an organization?

15. Which tool should be used first if performing an ethical hacking penetration test and why?

Current Version Date: 05/30/2011

Laboratory #6

Lab #6: Develop a Risk Mitigation Plan Outline for an IT Infrastructure

Learning Objectives and Outcomes

Upon completing this lab, students will be able to:

- Identify the scope for an IT risk mitigation plan focusing on the seven domains of a typical IT infrastructure

- Align the major parts of an IT risk mitigation plan within each of the seven domains of a typical IT infrastructure

- Define the tactical risk mitigation steps needed to remediate the identified risk, threats, and vulnerabilities commonly found in the seven domains of a typical IT infrastructure

- Define procedures and processes needed to maintain a security baseline definition for on-going risk mitigation within the seven domains of a typical IT infrastructure

- Create a table of contents for an IT risk mitigation plan encompassing the seven domains of a typical IT infrastructure

Required Setup and Tools

This is a paper-based lab and does not require the use of a "mock" IT infrastructure or virtualized server farm.

The standard Instructor and Student VM workstation with Microsoft Office 2007 or higher is required for this lab. Students will need access to their completed Lab #4 –Assessment Worksheet, Part A – Perform a Qualitative Risk Assessment for an IT Infrastructure prioritizing the risks, threats, and vulnerabilities identified from the qualitative risk assessment.

In addition, Microsoft Word is a required tool for the student to craft a table of contents for an IT risk mitigation plan and for answering and submitting the Lab #6 – Assessment Worksheet questions and answers.

Current Version Date: 05/30/2011

Recommended Procedures

Lab #6 – Student Steps:

Student steps needed to perform Lab #6 – Develop a Risk Mitigation Plan Outline for an IT Infrastructure:

1. Connect your removable hard drive or USB hard drive to a classroom workstation.

2. Boot up your classroom workstation and DHCP for an IP host address.

3. Login to your classroom workstation and enable Microsoft Word.

4. Obtain the results of your Lab #4 – Assessment Worksheet, Part A – Perform a Qualitative Risk Assessment for an IT Infrastructure.

5. Identify the scenario and vertical industry you were assigned in Lab #4:

    a. Healthcare provider under HIPPA compliance law

    b. Regional bank under GLBA compliance law

    c. Nationwide retailer under PCI DSS standard requirements

    d. Higher-education institution under FERPA compliance law

6. Review the results of your Lab #4 – Perform a Qualitative Risk Assessment for an IT infrastructure. Identify the prioritization of critical, major, and minor risk elements for the IT infrastructure

7. Organize your qualitative risk assessment data according to the following:

    • Review your executive summary from Lab #4 - Perform a Qualitative Risk Assessment for an IT infrastructure

    • Organize all critical "1" risks, threats, and vulnerabilities identified throughout the seven domains of a typical IT infrastructure

8. Conduct a high-level narrative discussion and review of the elements of an IT risk mitigation plan outline to consist of the following major topics/elements:

    a. Executive summary

    b. Prioritization of identified risks, threats, and vulnerabilities organized into the seven domains

    c. Critical "1" risks, threats, and vulnerabilities identified throughout the IT infrastructure

    d. Short-term remediation steps for critical "1" risks, threats, and vulnerabilities

    e. Long-term remediation steps for major "2" and minor "3" risks, threats, and vulnerabilities

    f. On-going IT risk mitigation steps for the seven domains of a typical IT infrastructure

    g. Cost magnitude estimates for work effort and security solutions

    h. Implementation plans for remediation

Current Version Date: 05/30/2011

9. Craft a detailed IT risk mitigation plan outline by inserting appropriate sub-topics and sub-bullets in the IT risk mitigation plan outline using the framework provided in step #8.

Deliverables

Upon completion of the Lab #6 – Develop a Risk Mitigation Plan Outline for an IT Infrastructure, students are required to provide the following deliverables:

1. Lab #6 – An IT risk management plan outline using the framework provided. Students are to insert appropriate details in the IT risk management plan outline to provide executive management with a clear picture of what, where, and how risks, threats, and vulnerabilities must be mitigated

2. Lab #6 - Assessment Questions and Answers

Evaluation Criteria and Rubrics

The following are the evaluation criteria and rubrics for Lab #6 that the students must perform:

1. Was the student able to relate the scope for an IT risk mitigation plan to the seven domains of a typical IT infrastructure? – [20%]

2. Was the student able to align the major parts of an IT risk mitigation plan within each of the seven domains of a typical IT infrastructure? – [20%]

3. Was the student able to define the tactical risk mitigation steps needed to remediate the identified risk, threats, and vulnerabilities commonly found in the seven domains of a typical IT infrastructure? – [20%]

4. Was the student able to define procedures and processes needed to maintain a security baseline definition for on-going risk mitigation within the seven domains of a typical IT infrastructure? – [20%]

5. Was the student able to create a table of contents for an IT risk mitigation plan encompassing the seven domains of a typical IT infrastructure? – [20%]

Current Version Date: 05/30/2011

Lab #6: Assessment Worksheet

Develop a Risk Mitigation Plan Outline for an IT Infrastructure

Course Name: _____

Student Name: _____

Instructor Name: _____

Lab Due Date: _____

Overview

After you have completed your qualitative risk assessment and identification of the critical "1" risks, threats, and vulnerabilities, mitigating them requires proper planning and communication to executive management. Students are required to craft a detailed IT risk management plan consisting of the following major topics and structure:

A. Executive summary

B. Prioritization of identified risks, threats, and vulnerabilities organized into the seven domains

C. Critical "1" risks, threats, and vulnerabilities identified throughout the IT infrastructure

D. Remediation steps for mitigating critical "1" risks, threats, and vulnerabilities

E. Remediation steps for mitigating major "2" and minor "3" risks, threats, and vulnerabilities

F. On-going IT risk mitigation steps for the seven domains of a typical IT infrastructure

G. Cost magnitude estimates for work effort and security solutions for the critical risks

H. Implementation plans for remediation of the critical risks

Current Version Date: 05/30/2011

Lab #6: Assessment Worksheet

Develop a Risk Mitigation Plan Outline for an IT Infrastructure

Course Name: _____

Student Name: _____

Instructor Name: _____

Lab Due Date: _____

Overview

After completing your IT risk mitigation plan outline, answer the following Lab #6 – Assessment Worksheet questions. These questions are specific to the IT risk mitigation plan outline you crafted as part of Lab #6 – Develop a Risk Mitigation Plan Outline for an IT Infrastructure.

Lab Assessment Questions

1. Why is it important to prioritize your IT infrastructure risks, threats, and vulnerabilities?

2. Based on your executive summary produced in Lab #4 – Perform a Qualitative Risk Assessment for an IT Infrastructure, what was the primary focus of your message to executive management?

3. Given the scenario for your IT risk mitigation plan, what influence did your scenario have on prioritizing your identified risks, threats, and vulnerabilities?

4. What risk mitigation solutions do you recommend for handling the following risk element? User inserts CDs and USB hard drives with personal photos, music, and videos on organization owned computers.

Current Version Date: 05/30/2011

5. What is a security baseline definition?

6. What questions do you have for executive management in order to finalize your IT risk mitigation plan?

7. What is the most important risk mitigation requirement you uncovered and want to communicate to executive management? In your opinion, why is this the most important risk mitigation requirement?

8. Based on your IT risk mitigation plan, what is the difference between short-term and long-term risk mitigation tasks and on-going duties?

9. Which of the seven domains of a typical IT infrastructure is easy to implement risk mitigation solutions but difficult to monitor and track effectiveness?

10. Which of the seven domains of a typical IT infrastructure usually contains privacy data within systems, servers, and databases?

11. Which of the seven domains of a typical IT infrastructure can access privacy data and also store it on local hard drives and disks?

12. Why is the Remote Access Domain the most risk prone of all within a typical IT infrastructure?

Current Version Date: 05/30/2011

13. When considering the implementation of software updates, software patches, and software fixes, why must you test this upgrade or software patch before you implement this as a risk mitigation tactic?

14. Are risk mitigation policies, standards, procedures, and guidelines needed as part of your long-term risk mitigation plan? Why or why not?

15. If an organization under a compliance law is not in compliance, how critical is it for your organization to mitigate this non-compliance risk element?

Current Version Date: 05/30/2011

Laboratory #7

Lab #7: Perform a Business Impact Analysis for a Mock IT Infrastructure

Learning Objectives and Outcomes

Upon completing this lab, students will be able to:

- Define the goal and objective of a Business Impact Analysis (BIA)

- Identify where a Business Impact Analysis (BIA) fits within a Business Continuity Plan (BCP)

- Identify mission critical applications and access to data requirements for a given scenario

- Perform a Business Impact Analysis (BIA) utilizing a qualitative assessment approach

- Create a Business Impact Analysis executive summary report for management

Required Setup and Tools

This is a paper-based lab and does not require the use of a "mock" IT infrastructure or virtualized server farm.

The standard Instructor and Student VM workstation with Microsoft Office 2007 or higher is required for this lab. Students will need access to their completed, Lab #4 –Assessment Worksheet, Part A – Perform a Qualitative Risk Assessment for an IT Infrastructure prioritizing the risks, threats, and vulnerabilities identified from the qualitative risk assessment.

In addition, Microsoft Word is a required tool for the student to craft a BIA utilizing a qualitative assessment approach to prioritize mission critical applications, data, and IT systems and elements that are required to maintain business continuity. An executive summary report is also required for management along with answering and submitting the Lab #7 – Assessment Worksheet questions.

Recommended Procedures

Lab #7 – Student Steps:

Student steps needed to perform Lab #7 - Perform a Business Impact Analysis for an IT Infrastructure:

1. Connect your removable hard drive or USB hard drive to a classroom workstation.
2. Boot up your classroom workstation and DHCP for an IP host address.
3. Login to your classroom workstation and enable Microsoft Word.
4. Review Figure 2 – "Mock" IT Infrastructure.

Current Version Date: 05/30/2011

5. Identify the scenario/vertical industry you were provided in Lab #4 - assigned by your Instructor:

    a. Healthcare provider under HIPPA compliance law

    b. Regional bank under GLBA compliance law

    c. Nationwide retailer under PCI DSS standard requirements

    d. Higher-education institution under FERPA compliance law

6. Conduct a BIA by assigning a qualitative business impact value for each identified business functions and operations: Critical, Major, or Minor or None.

7. From this prioritization, identify the IT systems, applications, and resources that are impacted.

8. Assess the recovery time objectives needed for the IT systems, applications, and resources.

9. Complete Lab #7 – Assessment Worksheet, Part A – BIA Process Flow Sheets and Part B – Assessment Questions.

10. Craft a four-paragraph executive summary according to the following outline:

    a. Goals and purpose of the BIA – unique to your scenario

    b. Summary of Findings – business functions and assessment

    c. Prioritizations – critical, major, and minor classifications

    d. IT systems and applications impacted - to support the defined recovery time objectives

11. Work on Lab #7 – Assessment Worksheet and Questions and submit with your executive summary.

Deliverables

Upon completion of Lab #7 - Perform a Business Impact Analysis for a Mock IT Infrastructure, students are required to provide the following deliverables as part of this lab:

1. Lab #7 – Assessment Worksheet, Part A - BIA of business functions and operations

2. Lab #7 – Assessment Worksheet, Part B - Business Impact Analysis Executive Summary

3. Lab #7 - Assessment Questions and Answers

Evaluation Criteria and Rubrics

The following are the evaluation criteria and rubrics for Lab #7 that the students must perform:

1. Was the student able to define the goal and objective of a Business Impact Analysis (BIA)? – [**20%**]

2. Was the student able to identify where a Business Impact Analysis (BIA) fits within a Business Continuity Plan (BCP)? – [**20%**]

Current Version Date: 05/30/2011

3. Was the student able to identify mission critical applications and access to data requirements for a given scenario? – [**20%**]

4. Was the student able to perform a Business Impact Analysis (BIA) utilizing a qualitative assessment approach? – [**20%**]

5. Was the student able to create a Business Impact Analysis executive summary report for management? – [**20%**]

Current Version Date: 05/30/2011

Lab #7: Assessment Worksheet

Part A – Perform a Business Impact Analysis for an IT Infrastructure

Course Name: _____

Student Name: _____

Instructor Name: _____

Lab Due Date: _____

Overview

When performing a BIA, you are trying to assess and align the affected IT systems, applications, and resources to their required recovery time objectives (RTOs). The prioritization of the identified mission critical business functions will define what IT systems, applications, and resources are impacted. The RTO will drive what kind of business continuity and recovery steps are needed to maintain IT operations within the specified time frames.

1. Perform a BIA assessment and fill in the following chart:

Business Function Or Process	Business Impact Factor	Recovery Time Objective	IT Systems/Apps Infrastructure Impacts
Internal and external voice communications with customers in real-time			
Internal and external e-mail communications with customers via store and forward messaging			
DNS – for internal and external IP communications			
Internet connectivity for e-mail and store and forward customer service			
Self-service website for customer access to information and personal account information			

Current Version Date: 05/30/2011

e-Commerce site for online customer purchases or scheduling 24x7x365			
Payroll and human resources for employees			
Real-time customer service via website, e-mail, or telephone requires CRM			
Network management and technical support			
Marketing and events			
Sales orders or customer/ student registration			
Remote branch office sales order entry to headquarters			
Voice and e-mail communications to remote branches			
Accounting and finance support: Accts payable, Accts receivable, etc.			

Part B – Craft a Business Impact Analysis Executive Summary

Craft a BIA executive summary, follow this structure and format:

  a. **Goals and purpose of the BIA** – unique to your scenario

  b. **Summary of Findings** – business functions and assessment

  c. **Prioritizations** – critical, major, and minor classifications

  d. **IT systems and applications impacted** - to support the defined recovery time objectives

Current Version Date: 05/30/2011

Lab #7: Assessment Worksheet

Perform a Business Impact Analysis for an IT Infrastructure

Course Name: _____

Student Name: _____

Instructor Name: _____

Lab Due Date: _____

Overview

After completing your BIA report for your scenario and IT infrastructure, answer the following Lab #7 – Assessment Worksheet questions. These questions are specific to your BIA you performed for your scenario and IT infrastructure. Justify your answers where needed.

Lab Assessment Questions

1. What is the goal and purpose of a BIA?

2. Why is a business impact analysis (BIA) an important first step in defining a business continuity plan (BCP)?

3. How does risk management and risk assessment relate to a business impact analysis for an IT infrastructure?

4. What is the definition of Recovery Time Objective (RTO)? Why is this important to define in an IT Security Policy Definition as part of the Business Impact Analysis (BIA) or Business Continuity Plan (BCP)?

Current Version Date: 05/30/2011

5. True or False - If the Recovery Point Objective (RPO) metric does not equal the Recovery Time Objective (RTO), you may potentially lose data or not have data backed-up to recover. This represents a gap in potential lost or unrecoverable data.

6. If you have an RPO of 0 hours – what does that mean?

7. What must you explain to executive management when defining RTO and RPO objectives for the BIA?

8. What questions do you have for executive management in order to finalize your BIA?

9. Why do customer service business functions typically have a short RTO and RPO maximum allowable time objective?

10. In order to craft back-up and recovery procedures, you need to review the IT systems, hardware, software and communications infrastructure needed to support business operations, functions and define how to maximize availability. This alignment of IT systems and components must be based on business operations, functions, and prioritizations. This prioritization is usually the result of a risk assessment and how those risks, threats, and vulnerabilities impact business operations and functions. What is the proper sequence of development and implementation for these following plans?

Business Continuity Plan   : _____

Disaster Recovery Plan   : _____

Risk Management Plan   : _____

Business Impact Analysis   : _____

Current Version Date: 05/30/2011

Laboratory #8

Lab #8: Develop an Outline for a Business Continuity Plan for an IT Infrastructure

Learning Objectives and Outcomes

Upon completing this lab, students will be able to:

- Define the goals and purpose of a Business Continuity Plan (BCP) for an IT infrastructure

- Align the Business Impact Analysis to define the scope of their BCP for an IT infrastructure

- Identify the major parts of a BCP unique to their scenario and IT infrastructure

- Develop a BCP outline for a given scenario and vertical industry

Required Setup and Tools

This is a paper-based lab and does not require the use of a "mock" IT infrastructure or virtualized server farm.

The standard Instructor and Student VM workstation with Microsoft Office 2007 or higher is required for this lab. Students will need access to their completed, Lab #8 –Assessment Worksheet, Part A – Business Continuity Plan Outline.

In addition, Microsoft Word is a required tool for the student to craft a BCP plan outline. Your outline must identify the major parts of a BCP unique to your given scenario and vertical industry. Incorporate the results of your BIA to identify what business functions and operations require continuity and recovery processes and procedures.

Recommended Procedures

Lab #8 – Student Steps:

Student steps needed to perform Lab #8 – Develop an Outline for a Business Continuity Plan for an IT Infrastructure:

1. Connect your removable hard drive or USB hard drive to a classroom workstation.
2. Boot up your classroom workstation and DHCP for an IP host address.
3. Login to your classroom workstation and enable Microsoft Word.
4. Review Figure 4 – "Mock" IT Infrastructure.

Current Version Date: 05/30/2011

5. Use the same scenario/vertical industry you were provided in Lab #7 – Perform a Business Impact Analysis for an IT Infrastructure assigned by your Instructor:

   a. Healthcare provider under HIPPA compliance law

   b. Regional bank under GLBA compliance law

   c. Nationwide retailer under PCI DSS standard requirements

   d. Higher-education institution under FERPA compliance law

6. Incorporate the following BCP sections and essential sub-topics in your outline:

   • Initiation of the BCP – Introduction, Definitions, BCP Organizational Structure, BCP Declaration, BCP Communications and Information Sharing, etc.

   • Business Impact Analysis – risk assessment and analysis prioritizing business functions and operations aligned to IT systems, applications, and resources

   • Business Continuity / Disaster Readiness / Recovery – RTO, RPO, business continuity benchmarks, disaster recovery planning (DRP as a sub-set of a BCP plan), recovery steps and procedures for mission critical IT systems, applications, and data

   • Develop & Implement the Plan – the plan is a living and breathing document that requires annual updates and change control revisions. Implementation and the instructions for how to engage the BCP are part of this section

   • Test & Update the Plan – the most important part of a BCP or DRP is to test the plan with a "mock" business continuity disruption or disaster scenario. Table-top reviews of the processes and procedures can be conducted to inform all BCP and DRP team members of their roles, responsibilities, and accountabilities

7. Work in groups of two or three as assigned by your Instructor. Develop your BCP outline for your given scenario using the results of Lab #7 – Perform a business Impact Analysis on an IT Infrastructure and the "mock" IT infrastructure as shown in Figure 4.

8. Complete Lab #8 – Assessment Worksheets, Part A – BCP Outline and Part B – Assessment Questions.

Deliverables

Upon completion of the Lab #8 – Develop an Outline for a Business Continuity Plan for an IT Infrastructure, students are required to provide the following deliverables as part of this lab:

1. Lab #8 – Assessment Worksheet, Part A – BCP Outline

2. Lab #8 - Assessment Worksheet, Part B – Assessment Questions and Answers

Current Version Date: 05/30/2011

Evaluation Criteria and Rubrics

The following are the evaluation criteria and rubrics for Lab #8 that the students must perform:

1. Was the student able to define the goals and purpose of a Business Continuity Plan (BCP) for an IT infrastructure? – [**25%**]

2. Was the student able to align the Business Impact Analysis to define the scope of their BCP for an IT infrastructure? – [**25%**]

3. Was the student able to identify the major parts of a BCP unique to their scenario and IT infrastructure? – [**25%**]

4. Was the student able to develop a BCP outline for a given scenario and vertical industry? – [**25%**]

Current Version Date: 05/30/2011

Lab #8: Assessment Worksheet

Part A – Develop an Outline for a Business Continuity Plan for an IT Infrastructure

Course Name: _____

Student Name: _____

Instructor Name: _____

Lab Due Date: _____

Overview

Using the results of Lab #7 – Perform a BIA on an IT Infrastructure, incorporate your BIA into your BCP plan scenario and vertical industry focus. Work in teams of two or three students as assigned by your Instructor. Craft a more detailed BCP outline only (not an entire BCP plan, etc.) based on the following:

Use the same scenario/vertical industry you were provided in Lab #7 – Perform a Business Impact Analysis for an IT Infrastructure assigned by your Instructor:

    a. Healthcare provider under HIPPA compliance law

    b. Regional bank under GLBA compliance law

    c. Nationwide retailer under PCI DSS standard requirements

    d. Higher-education institution under FERPA compliance law

Incorporate the following BCP sections and essential sub-topics in your outline:

- **Initiation of the BCP** – Introduction, Definitions, BCP Organizational Structure, BCP Declaration, BCP Communications and Information Sharing, etc.

- **Business Impact Analysis** – risk assessment and analysis prioritizing business functions and operations aligned to IT systems, applications, and resources.

- **Business Continuity / Disaster Readiness / Recovery** – RTO, RPO, business continuity benchmarks, disaster recovery planning (DRP as a sub-set of a BCP plan), recovery steps and procedures for mission critical IT systems, applications, and data.

- **Develop & Implement the Plan** – the plan is a living and breathing document that requires annual updates and change control revisions. Implementation and the instructions for how to engage the BCP are part of this section.

Current Version Date: 05/30/2011

- **Test & Update the Plan** – the most important part of a BCP or DRP is to test the plan with a "mock" business continuity disruption or disaster scenario. Table-top reviews of the processes and procedures can be conducted to inform all BCP and DRP team members of their roles, responsibilities, and accountabilities.

Lab #8: Assessment Worksheet

Part A – Develop an Outline for a Business Continuity Plan for an IT Infrastructure

{Insert Scenario and Vertical Industry Here}

I.   Initiation of the BCP

II.   Business Impact Analysis

III.   Business Continuity / Disaster Readiness / Recovery

IV.   Develop & Implement the Plan

V.   Test & Update the Plan

Current Version Date: 05/30/2011

Lab #8: Assessment Worksheet

Develop an Outline for a Business Continuity Plan for an IT Infrastructure

Course Name: _____

Student Name: _____

Instructor Name: _____

Lab Due Date: _____

Overview

After completing your BCP outline for your scenario and IT infrastructure, answer the following Lab #8 – Assessment Worksheet questions. These questions are specific to the BCP you performed for your scenario and IT infrastructure. Justify your answers where needed.

Lab Assessment Questions

1. How does a BCP help mitigate risk?

2. What kind of risk does a BCP help mitigate?

3. If you have business liability insurance, asset replacement insurance, and natural disaster insurance, do you still need a BCP or DRP? Why or why not?

4. From your scenario and BIA from Lab #7, what were the mission critical business functions and operations you identified? Is this the focus of your BCP?

5. What does a BIA help define for a BCP?

Current Version Date: 05/30/2011

6. Who should develop and participate in the BCP within an organization?

7. Why does disaster planning and disaster recovery belong in a BCP?

8. What is the purpose of having documented IT system, application, and data recovery procedures and steps?

9. Why must you include testing of the plan in your BCP?

10. How often should you update your BCP document?

11. Within your BCP outline, where will you find a list of prioritized business operations, functions, and processes?

12. Within your BCP outline, where will you find detailed back-up and system recovery information?

13. Within your BCP outline, where will you find a policy definition defining how to engage your BCP due to a major outage or disaster?

14. Within your BCP outline, where will you find a policy definition defining the resources that are needed to perform the tasks associated with BC or DR?

15. What is the purpose of testing your BCP and DRP procedures, back-ups, and recovery steps?

Current Version Date: 05/30/2011

Laboratory #9

Lab 9: Develop Disaster Recovery Back-up Procedures and Recovery Instructions

Learning Objectives and Outcomes

Upon completing this lab, students will be able to:

- Relate how to lower RTO with properly documented back-up and recovery steps

- Define a process of defining IT system and application recovery procedures

- Identify a back-up solution for saving all of your Lab Assessment Worksheets on an alternate system than your Student VM workstation and hard drive

- Test and validate your basic back-up and recovery procedures for saving your Lab Assessment Worksheets on an alternate system or solution other than your existing hard drive

- Test the back-up and recovery procedures for RTO compliance

Required Setup and Tools

This is a paper-based and does not require the use of a "mock" IT infrastructure or virtualized server farm.

The standard Instructor and Student VM workstation with Microsoft Office 2007 or higher is required for this lab along with Internet access to an external e-mail service used by the student.

In addition, Microsoft Word is a required tool for the student to craft back-up and recovery instructions for your data to an external source other than your hard drive.

Recommended Procedures

Lab #9 – Student Steps:

The following presents the steps needed to perform Lab #9 – Develop Disaster Recovery Back-up Procedures and Recovery Instructions:

1. Connect your removable hard drive or USB hard drive to a classroom workstation.
2. Boot up your classroom workstation and DHCP for an IP host address.
3. Login to your classroom workstation and enable Microsoft Word.
4. Make a back-up of all your Lab #1 - #8 Assessment Worksheets.
5. Attach them to an e-mail to your personal e-mail address.
6. Verify receipt and verify file integrity of the file attachments.

Current Version Date: 05/30/2011

7. Open the file attachments with Microsoft Word.

8. Document your Labs #1 - #8 Assessment Worksheets back-up and recovery procedures.

9. Test your back-up and recovery procedures as per your RTO.

10. Identify areas to lower your RTO.

11. Answer the Lab #9 – Assessment Questions.

Deliverables

Upon completion of Lab #9 – Develop Disaster Recovery Back-up Procedures and Recovery Instructions, students are required to provide the following deliverables as part of this lab:

1. Lab #9 – Documented back-up and recovery instructions for Labs #9 – Assessment Worksheet data recovery

2. Lab #9 - Assessment Questions and Answers

Evaluation Criteria and Rubrics

The following are the evaluation criteria and rubrics for Lab #9 – Develop Disaster Recovery Back-up Procedures and Recovery Instructions that the students must perform:

1. Was the student able to relate how to lower RTO with properly documented back-up and recovery steps? – [20%]

2. Was the student able to define a process of defining IT system and application recovery procedures? – [20%]

3. Was the student able to identify a back-up solution for saving all of your Lab Assessment Worksheets on an alternate system than your Student VM workstation and hard drive? – [20%]

4. Was the student able to test and validate your basic back-up and recovery procedures for saving your Lab Assessment Worksheets on an alternate system or solution other than your existing hard drive? – [20%]

5. Was the student able to test the back-up and recovery procedures for RTO compliance? – [20%]

Current Version Date: 05/30/2011

Lab #9: Assessment Worksheet

Part A – Develop Disaster Recovery Back-up Procedures and Recovery Instructions

The following are the steps required to perform Lab #9 – Develop Disaster Recovery Back-up Procedures and Recovery Instructions:

- **Objective** – Save Copies of all Your Lab #1 - #8 Assessment Worksheets to Your E-Mail Box (i.e., yahoomail, gmail, hotmail, etc.) as a Back-Up System.

- **Step #1:** Define an RTO for a Disaster Recovery Scenario where your Lab #1 - #8 Assessment Worksheet files got corrupted: 15 Minutes.

- **Step #2:** Identify Available Disk Storage Capacity on Your Personal E-mail Box.

- **Step #3:** Copy and Attach Lab #1 - #8 Assessment Worksheets Unzipped as E-mail Attachments to Your Personal E-Mail Box.

- **Step #4:** Send the E-mail with your Lab #1 - #8 Assessment Worksheets to Your Personal E-mail Box for Back-Up and Storage on an External Source.

- **Step #5:** Retrieve the E-mail and Open Each E-mail Attachment with Microsoft Word to Verify File Integrity.

- **Step #6:** Document Your Back-Up and Recovery Procedures.

- **Step #7:** Identify the Total Amount of Time Required to Recover and Install the Lab #1 - #8 Assessment Worksheets on Your Student VM Hard Drive and Verify File Integrity.

- **Step #8:** Did You Achieve Your RTO? What steps and procedures can you implement to help drive RTO even lower?

Note: The above steps are high-level. Very detailed instructions including login to e-mail systems and other procedures may be included.

Current Version Date: 05/30/2011

Lab #9: Assessment Worksheet

Develop Disaster Recovery Back-up Procedures and Recovery Instructions

Course Name: _____

Student Name: _____

Instructor Name: _____

Lab Due Date: _____

Overview

The most important task for a business continuity and disaster recovery plan is to document all identified mission critical IT systems, applications, and data recovery procedures. Fast recovery times for IT systems and applications are achievable with efficient and accurate recovery instructions. This lab has the students apply the same concepts of disaster recovery back-up procedures and recovery instructions to their own data.

Lab Assessment Questions

1. How does documented back-up and recovery procedures help achieve RTO?

2. True or False. To achieve an RTO of 0, you need 100% redundant, hot-stand-by infrastructure (i.e., IT system, application, and data, etc.).

3. What is most important when considering data back-up?

4. What is most important when considering data recovery?

5. What are the risks of using your external e-mail box as a back-up and data storage solution?

Current Version Date: 05/30/2011

6. Identify the Total Amount of Time Required to Recover and Install the Lab #9 Assessment Worksheets on Your Student VM Hard Drive and open the file in Microsoft Word to verify integrity. {Insert your timed RTO using your computer clock – following your documented instructions and steps}.

7. Did you achieve your RTO? What steps and procedures can you implement to help drive RTO even lower?

8. What are some recommendations for lowering the RTO for retrieval and access to the back-up data file?

9. If you drive RTO lower what must you do to streamline the procedure?

10. Why is documenting and testing critical to achieve a defined RTO?

11. Why is it a best practice for an organization to document its back-up and recovery steps for DR?

12. What can you do to cut down on the recovery time for accessing, copying, and recovering your Lab #1 – Lab #8 individual worksheets to help achieve the RTO?

13. What will encryption of a disk or data in storage do to the RTO definition when attempting to retrieve and recover clear-text data for production use?

14. How many total steps did your back-up and recovery procedures consist of for this Lab exercise? Are there any that can be combined or streamlined?

15. If the individual accessing the system for DR purposes was not familiar with the IT system and required system administrator login credentials, what additional step is required in the recovery phase?

Current Version Date: 05/30/2011

Laboratory #10

Lab #10: Create a CIRT Response Plan for a Typical IT Infrastructure

Learning Objectives and Outcomes

Upon completing this lab, students will be able to:

- Relate how a CIRT plan can help mitigate risks found within the seven domains of a typical IT infrastructure

- Identify where CIRT monitoring and security operations tasks occur throughout an IT infrastructure

- Identify security controls and security countermeasures to mitigate risk throughout the IT infrastructure and to aid in security incident response

- Create a CIRT response plan using the 6-step incident response methodology using the Mock IT Infrastructure

Required Setup and Tools

This is a paper-based lab and does not require the use of a "mock" IT infrastructure or virtualized server farm.

The standard Instructor and Student VM workstation with Microsoft Office 2007 or higher is required for this lab. Figure 6 – "Mock" IT Infrastructure will be used to represent our IT infrastructure.

In addition, Microsoft Word is a required tool for the student to craft a CIRT response plan strategy defining the roles and responsibilities of CIRT members throughout the seven domains of a typical IT infrastructure.

Recommended Procedures

Lab #10 – Student Steps:

Student steps needed to perform Lab #10 – Create a CIRT Response Plan for a Typical IT Infrastructure:

1. Connect your removable hard drive or USB hard drive to a classroom workstation.

2. Boot up your classroom workstation and DHCP for an IP host address.

3. Login to your classroom workstation and enable Microsoft Word.

Current Version Date: 05/30/2011

4. Refer to Figure 6 – "Mock" IT Infrastructure for Lab #10. Your CIRT response plan must address **one** of the following:

   • Internet ingress/egress at ASA_Student

   • Headquarters departmental VLANs on LAN Switch 1 and 2 with clear-text privacy data

   • Remote branch office locations connected through the WAN

   • Data center/server farm at ASA_Instructor

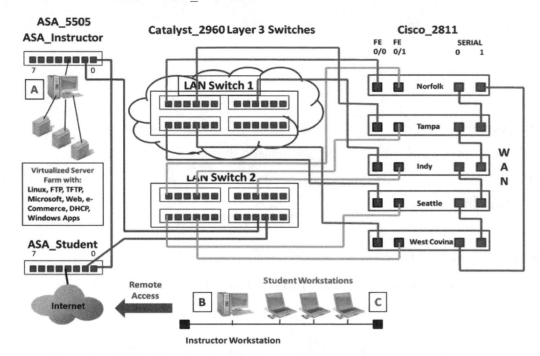

Figure 6 – "Mock" IT Infrastructure for Lab #10

5. For one of the above CIRT response plan items, build a CIRT response plan approach according to the defined 6-step methodology unique to the risks associated with the item:

   • **Step 1 – Preparation –** what tools, applications, laptops, and communication devices are needed to address computer/security incident response for this specific breach. Document this for this lab.

   • **Step 2 – Identification –** when an incident is reported it must be identified, classified, and documented. During this step, the following information is needed:

     1. Validating the incident

     2. Identifying its nature, if an incident has occurred

     3. Identifying and protecting the evidence

Current Version Date: 05/30/2011

4. Logging and reporting the event or incident

- **Step 3 – Containment** – the immediate objective is to limit the scope and magnitude of the computer/security-related incident as quickly as possible, rather than to allow the incident to continue in order to gain evidence for identifying and/or prosecuting the perpetrator. For the lab explain how you will solve this challenge.

- **Step 4 – Eradication** – the next priority is to remove the computer/security related incident or breach's affects. Explain what you would do for this lab.

- **Step 5 – Recovery** – recovery is specific to bringing back into production those IT systems, applications, and assets that were affected by the security-related incident. Define what your RTO would be for this lab and explain your reasoning.

- **Step 6 –Post-Mortem Review** – following up on an incident after the recovery tasks and services are completed is a critical last step in the overall methodology. A post-mortem report should include a complete explanation of the incident and the resolution and applicable configuration management, security countermeasures, and implementation recommendations to prevent the security incident or breach from occurring again

6. Identify security controls and security countermeasures you can implement throughout Figure 6 – "Mock" IT infrastructure to help mitigate risk from unauthorized access and access to intellectual property or customer privacy data

7. Answer the Lab #10 – Assessment Questions

Deliverables

Upon completion of Lab #10 – Create a CIRT Response Plan for a Typical IT Infrastructure students are required to provide the following deliverables as part of this lab:

1. Lab #10 – Documented CIRT response plan for one of four network points, Part A – Assessment Worksheet

2. Lab #10 - Assessment Questions and Answers

Current Version Date: 05/30/2011

Evaluation Criteria and Rubrics

The following are the evaluation criteria and rubrics for Lab #10 – Create a CIRT Response Plan for a Typical IT Infrastructure that the students must perform:

1. Was the student able to relate how a CIRT plan can help mitigate risks found within the seven domains of a typical IT infrastructure? – [**25%**]

2. Was the student able to identify where CIRT monitoring and security operations tasks occur throughout an IT infrastructure? – [**25%**]

3. Was the student able to select proper security controls and security countermeasures to mitigate risk throughout the IT infrastructure and to aid in security incident response? – [**25%**]

4. Was the student able to create a CIRT response plan using the 6-step incident response methodology using the Mock IT Infrastructure? –[**25%**]

Current Version Date: 05/30/2011

Lab #10: Assessment Worksheet

Part A – Create a CIRT Response Plan for a Typical IT Infrastructure

Overview

The following are the steps required to perform Lab #10 – Create a CIRT Response Plan for a Typical IT Infrastructure:

1. Refer to Figure 6 – "Mock" IT Infrastructure for Lab #10. Your CIRT response plan must address **one** of the following:

    *   Internet ingress/egress

    *   Headquarters departmental VLANs on LAN Switch 1 and 2 with clear-text privacy data

    *   Remote branch office locations connected through the WAN

    *   Data center/server farm

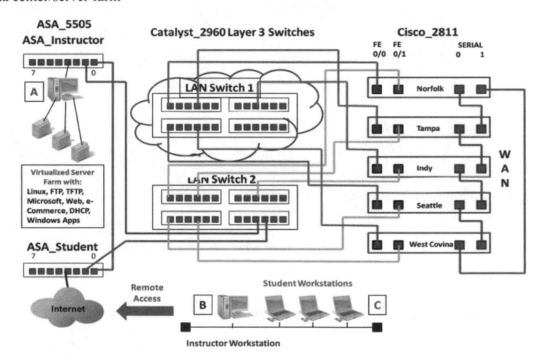

Figure 6 – "Mock" IT Infrastructure for Lab #10

2. For one of the above CIRT response plan items, build a CIRT response plan approach according to the defined 6-step methodology unique to the risks associated with the item:

Current Version Date: 05/30/2011

- **Step 1 – Preparation –** what tools, applications, laptops, and communication devices are needed to address computer/security incident response for this specific breach? Document this for this lab.

- **Step 2 – Identification –** when an incident is reported it must be identified, classified, and documented. During this step, the following information is needed:

  i. Validating the incident
  ii. Identifying its nature, if an incident has occurred
  iii. Identifying and protecting the evidence
  iv. Logging and reporting the event or incident

- **Step 3 – Containment –** the immediate objective is to limit the scope and magnitude of the computer/security-related incident as quickly as possible, rather than to allow the incident to continue in order to gain evidence for identifying and/or prosecuting the perpetrator. For the lab explain how you will solve this challenge.

- **Step 4 – Eradication –** the next priority is to remove the computer/security related incident or breach's affects. Explain what you would do for this lab.

- **Step 5 – Recovery –** recovery is specific to bringing back into production those IT systems, applications, and assets that were affected by the security-related incident. Define what your RTO would be for this lab and explain your reasoning.

- **Step 6 –Post-Mortem Review –** following up on an incident after the recovery tasks and services are completed is a critical last step in the overall methodology. A post-mortem report should include a complete explanation of the incident and the resolution and applicable configuration management, security countermeasures, and implementation recommendations to prevent the security incident or breach from occurring again. Explain what you would do port-mortem for an incident that occurs within your portion of the network.

Current Version Date: 05/30/2011

Lab #10: Assessment Worksheet

Create a CIRT Response Plan for a Typical IT Infrastructure

Course Name: _____

Student Name: _____

Instructor Name: _____

Lab Due Date: _____

Overview

The best risk mitigation strategy requires building and implementing a CIRT response plan. This means you are preparing for potential computer/security incidents and practicing how to handle these incidents. Like any kind of remediation, the more you can plan, prepare, and practice, the more prepared you are to handle any risk situation. This lab presented how to apply the computer/security incident response methodology to handling incidents specific to a portion of the network infrastructure.

Lab Assessment Questions

1. What risk mitigation security controls or security countermeasures do you recommend for the portion of the network that you built a CIRT response plan? Explain your answer.

2. How does a CIRT plan help an organization mitigate risk?

3. How does a CIRT response plan help mitigate risk?

4. How does the CIRT post-mortem review help mitigate risk?

5. Why is it a good idea to have a protocol analyzer as one of your incident response tools when examining IP LAN network performance or connectivity issues?

Current Version Date: 05/30/2011

6. Put the following in the proper sequence:

   Identification   :

   Containment   :

   Post-Mortem Review   :

   Eradication   :

   Preparation   :

   Recovery   :

7. Which step in the CIRT response methodology relates back to RTO for critical IT systems?

8. Which step in the CIRT response methodology requires proper handling of digital evidence?

9. Which step in the CIRT response methodology requires review with executive management?

10. Which step in the CIRT response methodology requires security applications and tools readiness?

Current Version Date: 05/30/2011